HIP-HOP INSIDER

HIP-HOP
MUSIC

By Marcia Amidon Lusted

CONTENT CONSULTANT

DAMON SAJNANI
ASSISTANT PROFESSOR, AFRICAN CULTURAL STUDIES
UNIVERSITY OF WISCONSIN–MADISON

Essential Library

An Imprint of Abdo Publishing | abdopublishing.com

Printed in the United States of America, North Mankato, Minnesota
042017
092017

 **THIS BOOK CONTAINS RECYCLED MATERIALS**

Cover Photo: Shutterstock Images
Interior Photos: Ray Tamarra/Everett Collection/Newscom, 5; Jemal Countess/ WireImage/Getty Images, 7; Debbie Wong/Shutterstock Images, 12; Christian Mueller/Shutterstock Images, 14–15; Allan Tannenbaum/Archive Photos/Getty Images, 17; Gilles Paire/Shutterstock Images, 20–21; PYMCAUIG Universal Images Group/Newscom, 24; Ken Babolocsay/ZumaPress/Newscom, 27; Andy Kropa// Invision/AP Images, 32–33; Tom Donoghue/Polaris/Newscom, 35; Anthony Behar/Sipa USA/Newscom, 37; Pablo Martinez Monsivais/AP Images, 45; Anthony Barboza/Archive Photos/Getty Images, 46–47; John Barrett/ZumaPress/ Newscom John Barrett/Globe Photos/ZumaPress/Newscom, 49; Jim Ruymen/ file photo UPI Photo Service/Newscom, 51; Jamie Lamor Thompson/Shutterstock Images, 56–57; Anthony Devlin/Press Association/URN:21702563/AP Images, 61; Granamour Weems Collection/Alamy, 62; RTNAtlas/MediaPunch/IPX/AP Images, 65; 2004 David G. McIntyre/Black Star/Newscom, 70–71; Jordan Strauss/Invision/ AP Images, 73; J. Stone/Shutterstock Images, 75; Alexis Simpson/ZumaPress/ Newscom, 79; Robert Altman/Polaris/Newscom, 81; Rudi Keuntje/Geisler- Fotopress/picture-alliance/dpa/AP Images, 83; Frank Micelotta/Invision/AP Images, 86–87; Sterling Munksgard/Shutterstock Images, 91; Matt Sayles/Invision/ AP Images, 94; Peter Jasinski/The Sentinel & Enterprise/AP Images, 96–97

Editor: Mirella Miller
Series Designer: Jake Nordby

Publisher's Cataloging-in-Publication Data
Names: Lusted, Marcia Amidon, author.
Title: Hip-hop music / by Marcia Amidon Lusted.
Description: Minneapolis, MN : Abdo Publishing, 2018. | Series: Hip-hop insider |
    Includes bibliographical references and index.
Identifiers: LCCN 2016962255 | ISBN 9781532110306 (lib. bdg.) |
    ISBN 9781680788150 (ebook)
Subjects: LCSH: Hip-hop--Juvenile literature. | Rap (Music)--Juvenile literature.
Classification: DDC 782--dc23
LC record available at http://lccn.loc.gov/2016962255

CONTENTS

1 THE BIRTH OF THE
SCRATCH

The year was 1975, and DJ Grand Wizard Theodore was a 12-year-old kid named Theodore Livingston, living in the Bronx borough of New York City. He practiced his deejaying skills and listened to music every day when he got home from school. In the late 1970s, DJs played vinyl records on two turntables and used audio mixers to smoothly transition songs from one to the other. Theodore came home one day as usual and started playing his music. What happened next changed hip-hop music forever:

> [On] this particular day I came home and played my music too loud and my mom was banging on the door and when she opened the door I turned the music down but the music was still playing in

Today DJ Grand Wizard Theodore teaches advanced classes in deejaying.

DJS AND EMCEES

In hip-hop music, unlike other forms of American music, the fundamental performers are not singers and bands but emcees and DJs. Rap is performed by the emcee over a background of music provided by the DJ. This music may be originally composed, but it may often make heavy use of sounds and music recorded from other disparate music genres. Often the DJ loops or reworks the original music. Rap artists are usually referred to as MCs or emcees (derived from the term *master of ceremonies* but in hip-hop culture often revised as *mic controller*). The term DJ, or deejay, is an acronym for *disc jockey*. These are the people who choose and play music on radio stations or at events. In hip-hop, an MC usually provides the rap vocals while the DJ mixes the music samples. In the early days of hip-hop, the DJ was the star, and the MC talked about him over the music. Eventually, the MC, who was doing the actual rapping, became the star.

my headphones and she was screaming "If you don't turn the music down you better turn it off" ... but I was still holding the record and moving it back and forth listening in my headphones and I thought "This really sounded [like] something.... interjecting another record with another record." And as time went by I experimented with it ... and soon it became scratching.[1]

Mixing and producing new music entirely by using turntables was not a new idea. Turntables themselves were the most popular way to listen to music at the time. They played vinyl records: as the turntable spun the record, a needle moved along the surface of the record in a groove,

By the mid-1980s, DJ Grand Wizard Theodore's scratching had become an important element that helped hip-hop music become successful.

which produced the sound of the music. DJs were people skilled at changing from one record to another to keep continuous music playing during a party or on a radio station, at a time before music was recorded digitally. Grand Wizard Theodore had learned and expanded on techniques created by hip-hop DJ Grandmaster Flash. He knew Grandmaster Flash because Theodore's brothers, Gene and Claudio, had been part of an early hip-hop duo called the L-Brothers, and they often performed with Flash. Theodore would go with his brothers to

GRAND WIZARD THEODORE

Theodore Livingston was born in the Bronx, New York, on March 5, 1963. He had four brothers and two sisters. Two of Theodore's brothers, Gene and Claudio, helped him enter the music business through their hip-hop duo, the L-Brothers. They also introduced him to Grandmaster Flash, who became Theodore's mentor. Theodore adopted the stage name Grand Wizard Theodore for his DJ career, which accelerated after he started the technique of scratching, an important element in hip-hop music. In 1979, he formed a group with rappers Waterbed Kev, Master Rob, Dot-A-Rock, Prince Whipper Whip, and Ruby Dee, called Grand Wizard Theodore and the Fantastic Five. In 1980, they had a hit song called "Can I Get a Soul Clap," which became a cult classic. They also appeared in the hip-hop film *Wild Style* in 1983. Theodore never received as much lasting fame as Grandmaster Flash, but in 1999 he appeared at the Rock and Roll Hall of Fame's hip-hop conference.

performances and stand on a milk crate to watch Flash as he used the turntables. Flash's techniques included the practice of cutting, in which two copies of the same record were spinning on two separate turntables. The DJ would then switch back and forth between them to loop or repeat a part of a song for as long as they wanted. But the technique of moving a record back and forth so the needle scratched the record's surface was unique. It created a new sound that was different from the recorded music. Theodore began calling himself Grand Wizard Theodore as he started working as a DJ, and he formed a group called Grand Wizard Theodore and the Fantastic Five. Once his scratching technique caught on, DJs expanded on it. They used mixing equipment and developed incredible hand-eye coordination for finding precise parts of a song and dropping the needle in that place on the record.

From the Inner City to the World

DJ Grand Wizard Theodore did not set out to change hip-hop music. He claims he developed his technique to be different from everyone else who was playing identical records in the same way. Theodore noted, "I played different records and was scratching the records and interjecting different records and needle dropping coz [*sic*] I also invented the 'needle drop' and basically I would just display my talents

GRANDMASTER FLASH

Grandmaster Flash was born Joseph Saddler on January 1, 1958, in Barbados. His family moved to the Bronx, and by the time he was a teenager, Saddler was spinning records as a DJ at neighborhood block parties and dances. At age 19, he was deejaying at local discos. He was perfecting his techniques in cutting, back-spinning, and phasing. Flash went on to work with the Furious Five, a group of rappers that included Melle Mel (Melvin Glover), Cowboy (Keith Wiggins), Kid Creole (Nathaniel Glover), Mr. Ness aka Scorpio (Eddie Morris), and Rahiem (Guy Williams). They began recording and appearing on the *Billboard* music charts. Their 1982 song "The Message" is one of hip-hop's most important singles. Grandmaster Flash continues to be one of hip-hop's most famous personalities.

HIP-HOP FASHION

The clothing worn by hip-hop and rap stars has changed with the times. At one point, there were many different urban-wear companies selling the clothing hip-hop artists wore as status symbols. These included labels such as Cross Colours, FUBU, Sean John, and Karl Kani. Urban wear was once a powerful fashion statement reflecting the tastes and culture of hip-hop. Some of mainstream hip-hop's most elite performers are now wearing upscale European designer clothing. New street-wear brands such as Hood By Air, Public School, and Off-White have their roots in urban wear but are more similar to luxury fashion labels.

when it was time to do a party."[2] But similar to hip-hop itself, which was born at neighborhood block parties in New York City in the early 1970s, scratching spread until it was a permanent piece of what made hip-hop its own genre.

As hip-hop slowly evolved, it moved out of inner-city New York and reached new audiences as it was played on radio stations. As a genre, hip-hop music also developed into many different subgroups including conscious rap, gangsta rap, and western and southern variations. As it grew, hip-hop milestones demonstrated how an entirely new genre was becoming more mainstream in the United States, and eventually, the world. In 1984, the first hip-hop radio station, KDAY in Los Angeles, California, helped spread this new type of music and made it popular beyond New York City. Soon, people were watching hip-hop music videos on MTV, listening to it on records and at concerts, and playing cassettes on huge, portable boom boxes.

Moving into the Mainstream

Hip-hop's journey to becoming mainstream music was slow at first, but once the genre started to grow, it developed rapidly. In 1981, the rock band Blondie incorporated a rap section in the song "Rapture." The music video for the song included cameo appearances by hip-hop artist Fab 5 Freddy, who is also mentioned in the song's lyrics along with Grandmaster Flash. In 1990, the cover of *Newsweek* magazine featured rap star Tone Lōc and articles about "rap rage" and how street-rhyme music had

MORE MILESTONES

Hip-hop had its first nomination at the 1986 Grammy Awards. Three years later, hip-hop received its own award category. The *Source* magazine launched in 1988 as the "bible" of hip-hop music, politics, and culture. In 2007, Grandmaster Flash and the Furious Five became the first hip-hop group to be inducted into the Rock and Roll Hall of Fame. In 2008, the future president of the United States paid tribute to the popularity of hip-hop. While campaigning for president, Barack Obama was asked a question about his debate with rival Hillary Clinton. Obama responded by brushing his shoulders off, a reference to the Jay Z song "Dirt off Your Shoulder," mixing politics and hip-hop culture. In May 2011, President Obama and his wife, Michelle, included the rapper Common in a White House poetry reading.

Hip-hop superstar Nicki Minaj breaks boundaries for women in the genre.

become universally popular. Hip-hop music and artists appeared in commercials for companies such as Swatch and Gap, as well as television shows such as *The Cosby Show*. During the 1980s and 1990s, rap musicians and hip-hop visual art, such as graffiti, appeared in movies and on awards shows.

Hip-hop as a musical genre is relatively new. Compared with many other genres, such as rock, jazz, and folk, it is a newcomer. Many hip-hop artists and scholars make a distinction between rap and hip-hop: rap is a type of music, but hip-hop is a culture that includes not only rap and hip-hop music, but also graffiti, break dancing, and fashion. As rapper KRS-One said, "Rap is something you do, Hip-hop is something you live."[3]

Hip-hop has given voice to people who feel they have been ignored by society, such as minorities living in inner cities and those who frequently experience crime and poverty. From the first house parties in the Bronx, where hip-hop was born, to its role in today's Black Lives Matter campaign, hip-hop has risen as a new musical form and become an important yet controversial vehicle for social commentary and political protest.

THE BRONX

The Bronx, a borough of New York City, is the birthplace of hip-hop music. At the time when hip-hop was born, in the 1970s, it was a place where violence and poverty were serious problems. Buildings were crumbling, landlords were known to set fires to get insurance benefits on their properties, and police, firefighting, health, and sanitation services were lacking. The construction of the Cross Bronx Expressway destroyed many of the area's ethnic neighborhoods, along with homes and jobs. The Bronx was a place with an energetic mix of people, including whites, Latinos, West Indians, and Africans. Hip-hop historian Marcus Reeves says, "When you have those conditions and . . . a group of people . . . trying to survive . . . and people getting tired of that, then you begin to have this growing new cultural movement that comes out of the gangs to counteract the violence . . . and the negativity that come out of gang cultures."[4] Hip-hop gave Bronx youth a voice and something other than mainstream and disco music through which to express themselves. It was about youth and creativity and celebrated their power against destruction.

2 THE ROOTS OF
HIP-HOP

Hip-hop was born in the 1970s. Popular mainstream music was making a transition from the protest songs of the 1960s, which often dealt with issues such as the antiwar movement and questioning authority, to the songs of the 1980s, which included more lighthearted party and dance music. Disco, punk rock, and New Wave music were popular in the 1970s. Progressive rock, which combined rock music with genres such as classical and opera, was a new genre. Funk music grew out of the rhythm and blues, jazz, and soul music of the 1960s, but with a heavier beat and psychedelic sounds.

Compared with the lighter, dance-oriented popular music, hip-hop could be a darker and

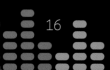

Hip-hop in the 1970s and 1980s was more than music. It also included fashion, art, and graffiti.

very different musical genre. It was closer to the rebellion songs of the 1960s, which protested the Vietnam War (1954–1975) and other social problems. It is important to recognize that hip-hop was not just music, but the cultural combination of multiple elements that were developing at the time: rapping, break dancing, graffiti, and turntablism.

Rooted in Tradition

Hip-hop music draws from many different musical and nonmusical traditions. The African tradition of oral storytelling and sharing history is one of the earliest forms of communication on which hip-hop draws. In cultures without written language, oral tradition is the only way to pass along history and culture from one generation to another. In West Africa, this tradition includes the creation of the first human, called Nommo. This is a myth of the Dogon people of Mali, West Africa, and dates back to approximately 3000 BCE. Nommo was

FROM POP TO SAMPLING

Many popular songs of the 1970s have been sampled and adapted by hip-hop artists:

- Ronnie Foster, "Mystic Brew"
- Timmy Thomas, "Why Can't We Live Together?"
- Isaac Hayes, "Joe Bell"
- James Brown, "The Payback"
- Parliament, "Give Up the Funk"
- The Isley Brothers, "Footsteps in the Dark"
- Bill Withers, "Grandma's Hands"
- Leon Haywood, "I Want'a Do Something Freaky to You"

created by Amma, the supreme god, and given the ability to use the spoken word. Nommo became a concept for words to create and act on people and objects, giving them life. This same concept of Nommo enables rappers to lift up African-American communities and voices through social commentary and music.

Rappers are also part of the African tradition of griots, who were respected oral historians and singers. They held tribal knowledge, including history, family connections, and news such as births, deaths, and wars, and shared it through the spoken word as they traveled from village to village. In the same way, rappers spread the news of their daily lives as well as the dreams and realities of their shared

BREAK DANCING

The term *break dancing* comes from the DJ turntable technique of the break beat. This stretches out a song's drum break by playing the drum portions of one song over and over, using two copies of the same record on two different turntables. This longer drum break provided more of an opportunity for dancing during the breaks. The dances performed during these breaks became known as break dancing. Break dancing includes movements such as waving or thrashing one's arms and legs, spinning on the top of one's head, arm balances, and bouncing one's back or stomach off the ground. Most break dancing is improvisational, meaning that the dancers are creating their own moves and routines to express themselves, but it takes great upper body strength, coordination, and rhythm to do it well.

Rappers have been compared to African griots because of their mutual use of oral traditions.

experiences. Through their songs and in performances, they share their own neighborhoods with those outside their areas. Some hip-hop scholars have compared the rappers to the griots, keeping track of modern working-class problems and histories, which are often different from what is seen in the mainstream media.

Modern-Day Griots

The modern technique of rapping was born from the verbal stylistics of African-American DJs on New York City radio stations in the late 1960s. These DJs introduced songs and artists in a rhyming, singsong style of speaking. They also included commentaries from their own lives and experiences, in a way that was similar to the griots of African tradition. Rap also draws from the rhyming games enslaved Africans developed

HIP-HOP VERSUS RAP

Hip-hop, as a type of music, is similar to but not the same as rap music. Hip-hop may include spoken rhythms and lyrics, but it can also be instrumental, with no vocals. Rap, on the other hand, always includes spoken vocal rhyming. Rap is an element of hip-hop culture as a whole, because it began when emcees would rhyme over the rhythms that the DJ created by mixing records and juggling breaks and beats.

before the American Civil War (1861–1865). These games allowed them to pass along their folklore and history in a way their white owners would not understand. These games also allowed slaves to use their creative abilities to tell stories about slaves escaping in a way that was disguised as innocent and comical. Slaves could share their experiences and comment on their world but not be punished as they would if they spoke in their own language or told stories in a way that demonstrated lack of respect for slaveholders.

These elements, drawn from African traditions, were important to the development of hip-hop. In addition to these older influences, hip-hop also incorporated many elements from other musical genres on top of new techniques, such as sampling, scratching, and using turntables and drum machines. The music itself, as well as the spoken elements, came from many kinds of music, performance poetry, and spoken word. Spoken word uses wordplay, tone, and voice to create a performance. As hip-hop pioneer Afrika Bambaataa said in a 1995 interview with the *Bomb Hip-Hop* magazine:

> *Hip-hop music is made up from other forms of music like funk, soul, rhythm & blues, jazz, rock, heavy metal, salsa, soca (calypso), TV shows, kiddie shows, horror movies, techno, pop, disco, African, Arabic, reggae etc. . . . the music is made by people from different races or nationalities from all over the planet, but its roots start with black people.[1]*

HIP-HOP'S CONSCIENCE

Rapper Lawrence Parker, known as KRS-One, is the leader of the hip-hop group Boogie Down Productions. The socially conscious group is concerned with spreading a message of antiviolence, especially after the death of founding member DJ Scott La Rock, who was gunned down in 1987 when he tried to break up a street fight. KRS-One named his fourth album "Edutainment," which describes his style of educating while entertaining. His songs address social issues. He routinely lectures at colleges on the history and philosophy of hip-hop. He even founded the Temple of Hip Hop, an organization dedicated to teaching hip-hop history.

Even though it drew on many rich traditions from Africa and from other types of music, hip-hop started small. It is commonly agreed hip-hop first appeared at

DJ Kool Herc was known for his massive sound system that played music so loudly, partygoers could feel the beat.

a birthday party held in an apartment building in the Bronx. The birthday girl's brother, Clive Campbell, would eventually become famous as DJ Kool Herc. He had been experimenting with turntablism and adding breaks to the music he was deejaying. He developed it after noticing how people reacted to the music he was playing. "I was noticing people used to wait for particular parts of the record to dance, maybe [to] do their specialty move," DJ Kool Herc later said.[2] This led him to perfect the technique of the break beat. His sister's party on August 11, 1973, brought together the biggest audience he had played for up to this point in his career. This birthday party helped launch a musical and cultural revolution and inspired others to develop it. Over the next ten years, hip-hop spread beyond the Bronx and into the mainstream.

THE OFFICIAL BIRTHPLACE

In 2007, the New York State Office of Parks, Recreation, and Historic Preservation officially recognized a West Bronx apartment building, located at 1520 Sedgwick Avenue, as the birthplace of hip-hop. The building is also eligible to be listed on the state and national registers of historic places. Buildings younger than 50 years old are not usually allowed on a historic register, but exceptions are made for buildings of "exceptional importance."[3] It was in the community room of this apartment building that DJ Kool Herc performed at his sister's birthday party.

3 MAINSTREAM MUSIC

It was October 13, 1979, and for the first time, a rap song had made it onto the *Billboard* music charts. These charts, published by *Billboard* magazine, use sales figures and radio station playlists to rank the most popular songs in a given week. The Sugarhill Gang's "Rapper's Delight" had been released one month earlier.

> *Now, what you hear is not a test I'm rappin' to the beat,*
> *And me, the groove, and my friends are gonna try to move your feet.*[1]

Before the song appeared on the charts, rap was something performed at parties and clubs, rather than recorded in a studio and released on records. In fact, many hip-hop artists did not

Members of the Sugarhill Gang gather at a magazine event in New York.

want to record their music. "Rapper's Delight" was the first hip-hop single. Since it received airtime on the radio, it introduced the sound of hip-hop to white listeners outside of the black neighborhoods where it had been born. It marks the point when hip-hop culture gave birth to the music genre.

A Golden Age

"Rapper's Delight" ushered in what is now known as hip-hop's golden age. This golden age spanned the 1980s and 1990s, when hip-hop became part of mainstream music. This was a time of innovation, diversity, and quality. Hip-hop was experimental, finding its place in the world, and expressing themes of African-American pride while also starting to explore political and social themes. *Rolling Stone* magazine called it a time "when it seemed like every new single [song] reinvented the genre."[2] Rappers were experimenting

A RELUCTANT HIT

The rap group Sugarhill Gang was not a real hip-hop group. It was assembled specifically for recording "Rapper's Delight." Sugar Hill Records founder Sylvia Robinson pulled together three artists, Big Bank Hank, Wonder Mike, and Master Gee, to record rhymes over an existing song. She created the group because she could not persuade any hip-hop emcees to record their own rhymes, since they all believed hip-hop should be performance music, not a recorded genre.

with techniques and ways to make their music innovative and interesting. They also had distinctive sounds that reflected their communities, and that had not yet been created through marketing strategies or in response to national trends. Hip-hop music was expanding beyond New York City and becoming popular in Los Angeles, California; Miami, Florida; and Detroit, Michigan.

The Birth of Rap Rock

One of the biggest hip-hop groups of the golden era was Run-D.M.C. The three members of the group were Joseph Simmons, known as Run, Darryl McDaniels, known as DMC (the initials of his name), and Jason Mizell, known as Jam Master Jay. They are regarded as one of the greatest rap groups in history. Instead of using music samples from funk and disco songs, as many rappers

RUN-D.M.C.

Run-D.M.C. was responsible for many firsts in the hip-hop music genre. In 1986, after having put out two albums, the group decided that one way to bring hip-hop music to a more mainstream audience was to create a collaboration with the rock group Aerosmith. The result was a remake of Aerosmith's song "Walk This Way." Run-D.M.C. was also the first rap group to have albums that went gold and platinum, meaning that they sold 500,000 (gold) or one million (platinum) copies.[3] It was the first rap group to appear on the cover of *Rolling Stone* magazine and to have a Top Ten single. And in 2016, it was the first rap group to receive a Grammy Lifetime Achievement Award.

"WALK THIS WAY"

In the 1980s, one of the surest ways to promote a song was by creating a video to go with it. Many of these videos aired on the television station MTV. The video for "Walk This Way" illustrates the birth of rap rock well. It shows Aerosmith and Run-D.M.C. rehearsing in adjacent studios. Then Run-D.M.C. begins rapping the lyrics to the Aerosmith song, and Aerosmith's lead singer, Steven Tyler, breaks through the wall between the studios and joins in. It physically illustrated the merging of hard rock and rap music.

were doing at the time, Run-D.M.C. used rock guitars, keyboards, and industrial sound effects in their music. They even collaborated with the rock group Aerosmith on a remixed version of Aerosmith's song "Walk This Way." The song helped Aerosmith's popularity and brought rap music to white audiences, whereas it had been considered an exclusively African-American trend before.

Run-D.M.C.'s collaboration with Aerosmith launched a new type of hip-hop called rap rock. Soon, more groups were crossing hard rock music with rap. The punk rock group Beastie Boys released an album, called *Licensed to Ill*, that was heavily influenced by rap music. The hip-hop group Public Enemy used samples from the rock group Slayer. In 1991, Public Enemy teamed with the rock group Anthrax to remix the song "Bring the Noise." Rap rock was popular throughout the 1990s.

Alternatives

Rap rock was not the only new type of hip-hop to surface during the golden age. For artists who did not want to conform to the dominant styles of rap music, there was alternative hip-hop, which drew from many different genres, including jazz, reggae, pop, soul, and even folk music. A few alternative groups, such as Arrested Development and the Fugees, crossed over into mainstream success, but others appealed mostly to listeners who enjoyed alternative rock rather than hip-hop or pop.

A group that crossed from hip-hop to pop music was Salt-N-Pepa. Cheryl "Salt" James and Sandy "Pepa" Denton were working in a store in Queens, New York City, when James's boyfriend asked them to rap on a song he was creating for a college class. The song, "The Show Stoppa," became a hit and the two women formed the group Salt-N-Pepa, eventually adding a third member, Deidra "DJ Spinderella" Roper. Their 1987 single "Push It" was one of the first rap songs

> "No one has been able to approach the political power that Public Enemy brought to hip-hop."[4]
>
> —Adam Yauch, Beastie Boys

Salt-N-Pepa broke the pattern of all-male hip-hop groups.

to be nominated for a Grammy Award. Salt-N-Pepa successfully bridged rap and pop music.

Music with a Conscience

The golden age of hip-hop also saw the beginning of socially conscious hip-hop music. Some artists used

their songs to challenge dominant social, political, and economic ideas. Their aim was to tell people about what was really going on in culture and politics, rather than what the mainstream media told the public. Because hip-hop was seen as a cool and trendy musical genre,

PUBLIC ENEMY

Public Enemy was both an extremely controversial rap group and one that created a version of hard-core rap music that was musically and politically revolutionary. Public Enemy was formed in 1982 by a group of friends studying at Adelphi University on Long Island, New York. Their lyrics rhymed about the social problems black communities faced and often seemed to encourage not only activism but also the use of revolutionary tactics. Their music included sampling that wasn't recognizable as the original songs, as well as the use of loud sirens, heavy backbeats, and funk. Their support of militant leaders such as black Muslim leader Louis Farrakhan, as well as some anti-Semitic comments made onstage during a performance, made them even more controversial. However, for their innovations in rap music, they were inducted into the Rock and Roll Hall of Fame in 2013.

this was a good way to inform listeners about issues such as racial and economic inequality. This kind of political statement had always been at the heart of hip-hop music, but socially conscious hip-hop artists gave it an even wider audience. Public Enemy criticized the US media, claiming rap music was the black version of the news, representing life in the inner city in a way that the mainstream media would and could not.

Socially conscious hip-hop paved the way for more aggressive hip-hop on social issues. As the genre spread to other major US cities, it spawned new types of hip-hop that addressed

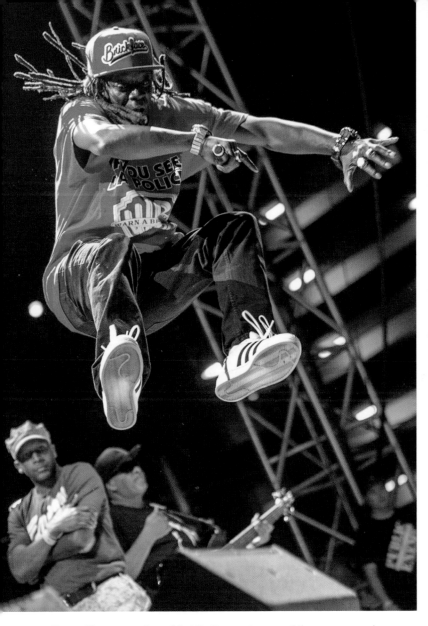

Flavor Flav, a member of Public Enemy, jumps while onstage as he performs with other members of the group at a festival.

issues even more directly and explicitly. People who felt ignored by modern society and politics were given a greater voice through hip-hop music and its strong lyrics.

4 HIP-HOP GOES
POLITICAL

Hip-hop was born in the inner city from the creative energies of young African Americans and later Latinos. It gave them a way to share their experiences and their communities and to entertain each other at parties and other neighborhood gatherings.

In 1982, Grandmaster Flash and the Furious Five released the song "The Message." It was immediately heralded as a landmark in the development of hip-hop's social consciousness:

> *I can't take the smell, can't take the noise . . .*
> *I tried to get away but I couldn't get far*
> *Cause a man with a tow truck repossessed*
> *my car[1]*

In the 1980s, hip-hop artists such as Grandmaster Flash became even stronger voices for people who felt marginalized.

The lyrics reflect the reality of a life plagued by drugs, crime, and poverty in the inner city, where disproportionate numbers of people suffer from discrimination and de facto racial segregation. "The Message" vividly narrates the everyday struggles of people who are offered few opportunities for education, employment, or advancement.

This new type of rap, which was sometimes called hard-core rap, started on the East Coast in the 1980s, but it soon spread to cities on the West Coast, such as Los Angeles. It was marked by emcees who began to minimize rapping about how good they were on the microphone and their DJs were on the turntables, and started rapping more about the gritty, harsh realities of urban life. Some groups taped their observations of actual life on the streets and used those recordings in their music. These songs had hard-driving

WU-TANG CLAN

One of the most innovative rap groups consisted of nine emcees who called themselves the Wu-Tang Clan. The group was named after mythological, invincible warriors with magical kung fu swords. The Wu-Tang Clan created a sound that was spare and minimal, with a heavy beat, long piano and string sections, and a sad, almost melancholy feeling. They topped the music with rap tracks that included martial arts themes, violence, and humor. The Wu-Tang Clan created a unique sound that was quickly imitated by other groups.

beats, and their lyrics talked about confrontation and aggression. It was streetwise music.

Gangsta Rap

Gangsta rap developed from hard-core rap toward the middle of the 1980s. It was also edgy and noisy and dealt with urban poverty and racism, but with increased emphasis on crime and drugs. The music covered subjects such as money, sex, violence, and drugs. The focus on crime-related subjects—and the gangsters who were involved in crime—was what made gangsta rap different from hard-core rap. It included crime stories that had supposedly happened, although sometimes the lyrics were exaggerations. Gangsta rap also romanticized the lives of these gangsters in a way that was exciting to young people, including middle-class white listeners. Gangsters had the same appeal as outlaws, as villains who defied law and order but also as heroes who stood up to the system and were tough and resourceful. There was also a certain glamour to violence and guns, which were not often a part of the daily lives of middle-class music fans. Because of its subject matter, gangsta rap was controversial, and many conservative groups around the United States tried to ban gangsta rap albums. This called nationwide attention to the social and political conditions in which people in the inner cities were living every day, giving these rappers a much bigger audience for their social commentaries.

West Coast Gangstas

Gangsta rap may have begun on the East Coast, but it was quickly taken over by gangsta rap in Los Angeles, which became a nationwide phenomenon. The rapper Ice-T was influential in developing gangsta rap, with his inflammatory lyrics and social commentary about life in South Central Los Angeles. Groups like N.W.A and Above the Law created songs that talked about sex, violence, and street crime in explicit terms that described the bleakness of life in the inner city. This ability to chronicle real life became a feature of Los Angeles gangsta rap. It was often combined with myths and the idea of immortality. These descriptions of such

NATIVE TONGUES

One collective of hip-hop artists, the Native Tongues, focused on sending a positive message in its songs and celebrating African cultures and ethnicities. The collective included several groups: A Tribe Called Quest, the Jungle Brothers, De La Soul, and Black Sheep. Their musical style was influenced by jazz beats and by sampling many different types of other musical styles. While the Native Tongues never released an album under that name, the groups associated with the Native Tongues are considered to be some of the most important in the development of hip-hop.

a difficult environment helped those who lived in the inner cities to feel some hope despite living in such dangerous conditions.

Los Angeles gangsta rap also became a voice for the tensions that existed between black and white neighborhoods. In 1988, N.W.A released the album *Straight Outta Compton*, which helped define the gangsta rap genre with its portrayal of violence, rebellion, and rage. Dr. Dre's 1992 record *The Chronic* and Ice-T's song "Cop Killer" spoke out against police brutality. Police often entered minority neighborhoods and broke down the doors of homes they suspected of drug activity. One rap's lyrics were:

NO GANGSTA RAP

There were several major US political and cultural figures who took a firm stance of disapproval toward gangsta rap. They included President George H. W. Bush and Tipper Gore (who was the wife of Senator and later Vice President Al Gore). C. DeLores Tucker, a famous civil rights figure, also spoke out against the profanity of gangsta rap and how it insulted women and African Americans. Reverend Calvin O. Butts, pastor of the Abyssinian Baptist Church in Harlem, went on a crusade against hard-core rap. He said, "You get to the point where you are constantly hearing, over and over, talk about mugging people, killing women, beating women, sexual behavior. When young people see this—14, 15, 16 years of age—they think this is acceptable behavior."[2]

ICE-T

Ice-T, whose real name is Tracy Marrow, was born in New Jersey but moved to Los Angeles at the age of 12 after his parents both died. His life in the inner city led him to his career as a rapper, and it also gave him credibility when he spoke against gang violence. He recorded the theme song for the film *Colors* in 1987, which centered on gangs. His 1991 album, *O.G. Original Gangster*, is said to have been one of the first to develop gangsta rap. His 1992 song "Cop Killer" was his most controversial, since it was seen as supporting violence against the police, although Ice-T said it was a commentary on police violence and racism against the black community. Ice-T has also appeared in many movies and television shows. He produced a reality show called *The Peacemaker: L.A. Gang Wars*, about real-life gang mediator Malik Spellman. Ice-T is committed to ending violence in the neighborhoods in which he grew up.

Well, I know to you we all look the same
But I'm not the one slingin' caine
I work nine to five and ain't a damn thing changed . . .[3]

Rap songs that dealt with the grim conditions in black neighborhoods around Los Angeles became the sound track for race riots that took place there in 1992. The potential for rioting was forewarned on Ice Cube's album *Death Certificate*, released in October 1991, and the riots, in turn, called even more attention to this kind of music and helped gangsta rap become mainstream more quickly. Artists such as Snoop Dogg and Tupac Shakur were signed to record labels at this time. And as soon as the Los Angeles riots ended, rappers were creating new songs about them. While gangsta rap's popularity eventually led to it becoming watered down and more about money and possessions than racial tensions, it gave an important perspective to the events of 1992.

Gangsta rap was blamed for racial unrest. More-conservative Americans also blamed it for desensitizing teenagers to guns, drugs, and gangs and urging them to commit violence. But it was a voice for those who were caught up in situations in which these things were a part of daily life.

THE LOS ANGELES RACE RIOTS

On April 29, 1992, four Los Angeles police officers were found innocent of any wrongdoing after an amateur video captured them beating an unarmed African-American motorist named Rodney King during a traffic stop. Just hours after this verdict, protests erupted and riots began in South Central Los Angeles. Rioters blocked traffic on the freeways, beat motorists, looted stores, and set fires. The police were slow to respond, and the violence spread across the city. President George H. W. Bush finally ordered federal officers and military troops into the city. By the time the riots ended three days later, 55 people were dead, 2,000 were injured, and more than $1 billion in property damage had occurred, including the burning of 4,000 buildings.[4] A federal jury eventually convicted two of the police officers for unreasonable use of force.

Rap and the Nation

Eventually, as the 1980s became the 1990s, nation-conscious rap evolved. Developing at the same time as gangsta rap, this rap was also socially conscious and political, but instead of demanding action and expressing aggression through guns and violence, it presented strong political messages and left the listeners to form their own opinions. Nation-conscious rap dealt with issues such as religion, African culture, the economy, fighting crime and violence, and the struggles of everyday people. This kind of hip-hop was especially important because many younger African Americans were disillusioned with standard politics and politicians and were looking for new leadership. For young people listening to rap, they were concerned with education, job opportunities, better relationships with the police, and reform of the criminal justice system. They were more apt to listen to and find ideas from rap DJs and emcees than from traditional politicians or black leaders. They could find their social activism in their music.

Some hip-hop artists, including Mary J. Blige, participate in social activism by performing at political fund raisers and events.

BEHIND
THE SONG

"THE MESSAGE"

A child is born with no state of mind

Blind to the ways of mankind . . .

You'll grow in the ghetto livin' second-rate

And your eyes will sing a song called deep hate... [6]

In 1982, Grandmaster Flash and the Furious Five released a
song called "The Message." It was one of the first songs in
which a well-known rap group voiced something important
about the culture hip-hop had come from. The lyrics describe
what it was like to live in the South Bronx of New York City
in the 1970s: decay, poverty, drugs, prostitution, violence,
and the possibility of dying young. Grandmaster Flash said
in a 1983 interview that the song showed he and his group
could "speak things that have social significance and truth." [7]
The song was slower and had a more serious subject matter
than many rap songs, but it was still commercially popular
and peaked at Number 4 on *Billboard*'s R&B singles chart.
Grandmaster Flash and the Furious Five did not survive as a
group, but they were inducted into the Rock and Roll Hall of
Fame in 2007, the first rap group to be so honored.

hip-hop groups to bring awareness to certain social issues.

5 EAST COAST VERSUS WEST COAS

The divide between geographical types of hip-hop was growing. There were many more cities and regions developing their own uniq and distinct types of hip-hop music. For mos of the 1990s, the rivalry between the East Coast and the West Coast hip-hop artists was more of a feud. One of the most visible playe in this feud was East Coast rapper Notorious B.I.G., signed to a New York City record label called Bad Boy Records, which was owned by rapper and producer Sean "Puff Daddy" Combs. On the West Coast was Tupac Shakur, on a Los Angeles–based record label called Death Row Records. This feud culminated in t shooting deaths of Shakur in Las Vegas, Neva in 1996 and Notorious B.I.G. one year later.

TUPAC SHAKUR

Tupac Shakur was one of the leading names in gangsta rap in the 1990s. He was born in New York City but ended up living on the West Coast. His parents, Billy Garland and Afeni Shakur, were both members of the Black Panther Party, a revolutionary organization originally started to protect blacks from police brutality in their own neighborhoods. When he was a teen, he sold drugs on the streets of San Francisco, California. He served eight months in prison for assault. This provided him with material for his rap music, which was known for being explicit, violent, and controversial. He also acted in several movies and released best-selling albums until September 7, 1996, when he was fatally shot. His killer has never been found. However, his legacy as a gangsta rap artist continues. In 2012, during a concert with Dr. Dre and Snoop Dogg, his seemingly three-dimensional image was projected onstage to perform.

What exactly was this feud and rivalry about? Each coast was developing its own unique sound and fighting for the biggest share of popularity and the money that came with it. The violence of these two rappers' deaths brought the gradual decline of the East Coast–West Coast feud and the rise of more mainstream types of hip-hop.

The New West

At first, West Coast rap seemed to echo the original, harder rap sound that originated in New York City. But during the 1990s, West Coast rap began creating its own sounds. In addition to the gangsta style rap of Ice-T, there was Latin-inspired

Rapper Tupac Shakur was killed before he was able to see the extent of his success as a hip-hop artist.

and the lighter sound of the Pharcyde. M.C. Hammer combined rap with pop. Dr. Dre pioneered G-funk, which was hip-hop with a distinctive, whiny synthesizer sound, a deep bass, and often female voices singing background. G-funk became one of the most popular types of hip-hop of the decade. But West Coast hip-hop was just as varied and hard to define as the East Coast styles until the group N.W.A emerged in the late 1980s. It created a harder sound that combined social commentary with lyrics about violence and living for good times, which was taken up by other West Coast artists. Death Row Records, with artists such as Snoop Dogg, Dr. Dre (a former member of N.W.A), and Tupac Shakur, became popular nationally. There was continuing controversy, however, with West Coast rap, especially the way it glorified partying, drugs, and sex. Shakur often commented on the feud between East and West Coast rap communities in his lyrics, insulting his enemies. There were also complaints about how West Coast rap portrayed women, treating them largely as sexual objects and discounting them as people.

Meanwhile, back on the East Coast, hip-hop artists were also creating new kinds of sounds. East Coast hip-hop had declined with the increased popularity of the West Coast styles, but in the late 1990s it experienced a rebirth, bringing back hard-core hip-hop. One album, *Illmatic* by Nas, is still considered to be one of the best hip-hop albums. *Illmatic* helped recreate East Coast hip-hop. It combined a sophisticated jazz beat with lyrics about the reality of inner-city life but also about the good times and hope for the future.

Jay Z, the Roots, MF Doom, Eminem, and 50 Cent became popular in the late 1990s. As listeners moved away from the gangsta rap of the West Coast, East Coast hip-hop became more entwined with pop music. It became more about big business and record sales and less about its roots as a voice for forgotten urban youth. Hip-hop elements, such as rhyming lyrics and sampling,

DEATH ROW RECORDS

Death Row Records was an entertainment company started in Los Angeles in 1991. It was born largely because rap artists were creating songs that were making millions of dollars for their record companies, but often receiving very little in pay themselves. To end what they saw as exploitation, a group of rappers from Compton, California, led by Dr. Dre and the D.O.C., decided to start a label, Death Row Records, and have control over the music and finances. Death Row Records was eventually making $100 million a year until the death of Tupac Shakur, one of the label's artists.[1] The FBI also investigated the company for possible relationships between its financial backers and drug traffickers. By 2006, the company declared bankruptcy, and in 2009 it was auctioned off to another company.

JAY Z

Jay Z was born Shawn Corey Carter in New York City. He recorded his first rap single in 1989 as a duo with rapper Jaz-O. As a result, they appeared on the television show *Yo! MTV Raps*. In 1996, with two friends, Damon Dash and Kareem Burke, Jay Z started the Roc-A-Fella record label and released his first album. Since then, he has also created an entertainment company called Roc Nation, which represents many well-known musicians, including Kanye West. Jay Z has a clothing line called Rocawear and a film company, Roc-A-Fella Films. He has performed for charitable and political causes, and caused some controversy during the 2016 presidential campaign when he performed at a benefit concert for Hillary Clinton that included songs with explicit lyrics. He is married to singer and actress Beyoncé.

were finding their way into many other types of music, including neo-soul, which combined soul music with rap, as well as rapcore and rap metal (a combination of rap, heavy metal, and punk). Groups performing in these new genres included Limp Bizkit and Rage Against the Machine.

A New Southern Sound

Hip-hop was never just limited to the East and West Coasts. New artists in other regions were making their voices heard. Southern rap first began making an appearance with the Geto Boys from Houston, Texas, in 1986; Arrested Development from Atlanta, Georgia; and the Nolimit Posse from New Orleans, Louisiana. All of these groups became popular around the country.

Southern rap music created its own subgenre called crunk. People who went to hear music in Atlanta's clubs used the term to describe energetic, fun music. Crunk became famous as a new Southern hip-hop genre, which combined hip-hop with electronic dance music. It was music for clubs, and the songs were high-pitched and used heavy drumbeats. The lyrics included catchy refrains that repeated often so the audience could chant along with the music. Crunk rappers usually shouted or screamed their lyrics aggressively, and sometimes the songs used a call-and-response style, in which the artist would shout a line and the audience would scream a line back in response.

Crunk was often criticized for not having a lot of substance or message, but it was meant to be fun and stylish. Crunk became popular nationally in 2003, when Lil Jon & the East Side Boyz's song "Get Low" appeared on national music charts. Other crunk artists included Three 6 Mafia, Ying Yang Twins, Lil Scrappy, and YoungBloodZ. Crunk also had its own subgenres, including crunkcore, crunk rock, crunk punk,

"Personally, I just think rap music is the best thing out there, period. . . . That's all I buy, that's all I live, that's all I listen to, that's all I love."[2]

—Eminem

Young Jeezy performs a call-and-response song with the crowd in Atlanta, Georgia.

crunk R&B, and acid crunk, all of which combined crunk with more-established types of music.

Trapping and Snapping

Another type of Southern rap that became popular was trap music. It started in Atlanta, where groups such as Ghetto Mafia and Dungeon Family used the term to describe their sound. It included a distinctive beat that used kick drums, hi-hat cymbals, and a great deal of synthesizer sound. The term *trap* came from street slang. A trap was a drug house where narcotics were made and sold. Trap rappers usually sang about drugs. Unlike crunk music, trap lyrics talked about life on the streets and the bleak standard of living there. But nonetheless trap music was popular party music. Young Jeezy and T.I. were two

CRUNK EVERYWHERE

Crunk became popular as party music, especially on college campuses. People had crunk ringtones on their phones, and crunk could be heard on the radio, on car stereos, and in nightclubs. There was even an energy drink called Crunk Energy. Crunk was so popular largely because it was party music and listeners linked it to having a good time, but it also had undertones of partying as a way to release pain. The term *crunk* itself supposedly comes from combining the words *chronic* and *drunk*, implying that the music was meant to go along with the constant partying that people did to forget their troubles. *Chronic* means ongoing or all of the time, but it also refers to marijuana. Crunk's heavy bass beat and repetitive lyrics were meant for dancing and drinking.

artists who made trap music popular and even helped it cross over onto mainstream radio stations. While crunk music declined through the 2000s, trap rap has remained popular into the 2010s.

An outgrowth of crunk was a music type called snap, which relied on finger snapping to take the place of a snare drum sound. It had a slower tempo than crunk, but it still talked about clubs, strippers, and other party topics. The group D4L's song "Laffy Taffy" was the most well-known snap song. Dem Franchize Boyz and Fabo were also groups that pioneered the snap music sound. Snap music has its own four specific dances done in clubs, with the DJ instructing the dancers on how to do each dance. The specific dances are the Poole Palace, the Westside Walk, Jocin', and the

Snap Dance. They are very simple dances, but different snap artists have different ways of teaching them. They are similar to square and line dances, in which a caller tells the dancers what steps to do and how to move. Snap dances included moving the torso and arms while barely moving the feet, then leaning back and finger snapping to the music.

Hip-hop in the United States started in New York City and spread to California and cities in between. By the beginning of the 2000s, many new genres of hip-hop and new sounds developed, and hip-hop itself had become a mainstream type of music. Soon, hip-hop would leave the boundaries of its home country and become a worldwide music style as well.

6 WORLD MUSIC

Hip-hop had become an accepted, mainstream type of music in the United States. So it was to be expected that it would also start spreading around the world, especially as the Internet and digital music sharing became more common in the 2000s. Soon, hip-hop was not limited to vinyl records and live party performances. It was also finding its voice with other artists in other countries.

One of the first countries hip-hop traveled to in the late 1970s and early 1980s was the United Kingdom. The record "Rapper's Delight" from the Sugarhill Gang made it onto the UK record charts in 1979. It brought attention to hip-hop there and found many new fans. Hip-hop also

UK hip-hop artist Clement Marfo performs in London in 2014.

The film *Beat Street* brought attention to hip-hop, making the new musical genre increasingly popular in the United Kingdom.

made its way across the world through radio shows, mixtapes, and albums. Hip-hop culture gained an even better foothold in other countries because of two US hip-hop films: *Wild Style* in 1983 and *Beat Street* in 1984. Just as in the United States, hip-hop groups in the United Kingdom started in clubs and at parties, where music was played live.

Hip-hop in the United States gave a voice to marginalized and oppressed people across the country. The same thing happened in the United Kingdom, where there were many migrants who had come in search of jobs, especially from former British colonies, and were faced with racial discrimination. Many young migrants found their own identity in hip-hop music. This happened especially in London, which had a strong music industry and many outlets for hip-hop to be heard and spread, either live or through specialty record shops and homemade mixtapes. London was at the forefront because its minorities were not usually living in separate areas. Instead, they lived in racially mixed neighborhoods where there were more cultural exchanges between people from all around the world.

British hip-hop artists such as London Posse, the Cookie Crew, Monie Love, and Ruthless Rap Assassins started out imitating the US hip-hop sound, even using American accents in their raps. But eventually UK hip-hop found its own unique sound with its own meanings and musical influences. In the 1990s, UK hip-hop began developing regional differences in sound. British hip-hop had its own radio stations and magazines. Hip-hop's popularity in England dipped slightly in the early 2000s but revived with the establishment of the High Focus Records label in 2010, dedicated to providing a platform for a new generation of UK artists and producers. Some of today's best-known UK rappers include Fliptrix, Jam Baxter, and Chester P. Hip-hop artists are finding new ways to reach listeners through social networking sites and YouTube.

Hip-Hop Ambassadors

Hip-hop also spread outside the United States because of some celebrity US rappers. When Afrika Bambaataa released his single "Planet Rock" in 1982, it used musical ideas from German electropop, British rock, and African-American disco rap. The blend of different musical cultures made the song popular all around the world, and that same year, Bambaataa went on the first hip-hop music tour outside of the United States. His tour spread the word about hip-hop music everywhere he went in Europe, Africa, and Asia and started hip-hop movements in many other countries. The rap group Public Enemy also went on worldwide musical tours, and its visit to Brazil in the late 1980s resulted in an explosion of hip-hop in Latin America. For black people in some of these countries, US rap was a reminder of how music could be a voice for expression, power, and change.

Afrika Bambaataa quickly became a leader in the New York hip-hop community.

65

MC SOLAAR

When Afrika Bambaataa toured in Europe, his performances inspired the artist who would become the first non-American rap superstar. MC Solaar was born in Senegal, but was living in Paris, France, as a young teenager. He had already discovered the music of Bambaataa, and had begun making his own rap music. MC Solaar is known for his complex lyrics and his use of wordplay in French. Because he had a multicultural background, he appealed to many young music fans in France, which soon became the biggest market for non-English-speaking rap music. In turn, he had a hand in bringing Senegal's first major hip-hop act, Positive Black Soul, to worldwide acclaim in the early 1990s. Didier Awadi, one of PBS's emcees, remains the most prominent rapper across Francophone West Africa.

Hip-hop music was able to spread so quickly and become so popular in other parts of the world in part because of cable and satellite television. In 1988, the MTV music channel created a program in the United States called *Yo! MTV Raps*, which showed hip-hop videos. The program showcased African-American and Latino hip-hop music, and soon it was not only watched across the United States but also televised globally, first in Europe and then on MTV Asia and MTV Latin America.

Hip-hop remained a voice for oppressed people a way for them to express themselves to powerful people, even after hip-hop became more commercial and less political in the United States. In both the United Kingdom and France, there have been battles between governments and hip-hop fans as hip-hop culture clashed with mainstream values in those countries. However, as American hip-hop has become more popular around the world—and more commercial, with an increased emphasis on selling products—it has pushed local rappers and musicians in Africa, Asia, the Caribbean, and South America and their experimental types of hip-hop off the radio and television stations.

Hip-Hop Goes to China

As early as the 1990s, US rappers such as Eminem and Q-Tip were popular in China, but it was not until the 2000s that China had its own rappers. Hip-hop music has become very popular with young Chinese listeners, even though it is not sanctioned by the government and has not been allowed on mainstream broadcast media. It has been largely an underground musical genre because it expresses discontent with the Chinese Communist system, something the government does not allow. Communism limits free expression, and hip-hop by its nature is a

> "Everybody needs to show respect to each other's ways and the cultural life that you get on this planet. Don't get caught up on 'I'm brown, black, white, red, blue, whatever.' . . . All these names we're using now are just an illusion made to keep us fighting each other."[1]
>
> —Afrika Bambaataa

HIP-HOP AND THE ARAB SPRING

In 2010, a series of political uprisings began across Egypt, the Middle East, and North Africa. They came to be known as the Arab Spring. Hip-hop played an important role in the Arab Spring as a way for those people who were dissatisfied with their governments to give voice to their protests and share their cultures. The Tunisian hip-hop artist El Général released a hip-hop song called "Rais Lebled," which means "president of the country." In the song, he is pleading with the president of Tunisia to pay attention to Tunisian youth who were very smart and well-educated but could not find jobs. This song and others that followed inspired protesters who wanted freedom and change. El Général was arrested and tortured, but his music continued to be a call to action in the streets and on the Internet.

type of music that speaks out against existing social systems. Wang Liang, a popular hip-hop DJ in China who is known as Wordy, thinks of hip-hop as a free kind of music that allows people to express what they are thinking and feeling. He said, "The Chinese education system doesn't encourage you to express your own character. They feed you stale rules developed from books passed down over thousands of years. There's not much opportunity for personal expression or thought; difference is discouraged."[2] Chinese fans once listened to hip-hop in English, which most of them could not understand, until groups such as Yin Ts'ang began writing hip-hop lyrics in Chinese. Since then, hip-hop has grown in China, and there are hip-hop clubs opening in cities all over the country, as well as thousands of Chinese raps and videos on the Internet.

There is an annual rap event called Iron Mic that takes place in Shanghai every year. In these battles, rappers take the stage together and compete to make improvised rhymes in more than one language to the music that a DJ spins. Sometimes this leads to an actual language battle, with one artist scolding another for not speaking in proper Mandarin Chinese and another claiming that to speak only Mandarin and not English or Cantonese is disrespecting regular people.

International companies, such as Intel, Coca-Cola, and Adidas, use hip-hop and Chinese rappers to

SPREADING THE MESSAGE WITH HIP-HOP

The Chinese government has changed its stance on rap music, realizing that it can be used as a way to get certain messages across to young people. In 2016, Chinese state media actually promoted a rap song about Karl Marx, whose work *The Communist Manifesto* is a foundation for communist thinking. The government's newspaper stated that a rap song about Marx, called "Marx Is a Post-90," shows that his ideas still appeal to young people and will never go out of style. *Post-90* is China's term for young people in the millennial age-group. However, rap songs that seem to promote drugs, violence, and other negative behaviors are still censored by the Chinese Communist government.

MC Sbazzo performs in Beijing, China, in an underground hip-hop club.

market their goods to Chinese teens. However, China's Ministry of Culture routinely bans many hip-hop songs, saying they harm social morality and Chinese culture. The Chinese government does not tolerate the themes of sex, rebellion, and violence that are a big part of hip-hop music, and it often blacklists artists who make this kind of music, which means these artists cannot easily distribute

their music or perform in public. This kind of suppression only makes hip-hop stronger as a voice of the people.

As hip-hop becomes a global musical genre, it crosses the barriers of language, culture, race, and governments in a way most other social forms have not. And because of its globalization, new types of hip-hop are being created in other countries. Hip-hop continues to evolve.

7 NEW HIP-HOP

Hip-hop music in general had evolved from a small, local type of music into a mainstream, worldwide genre. Many of its biggest stars were making millions of dollars and living celebrity lifestyles, far removed from the urban experience that had created hip-hop in the first place. With the beginning of the new millennium in 2000, there were hip-hop artists who still cared about exploring and developing new forms of hip-hop and using different methods to reach their listeners.

Back Under Again

Hip-hop began as underground music, not part of the mainstream commercial music industry. After much of hip-hop's move to broader

With his Southern sound, Lil Wayne was one of the most iconic hip-hop artists of the 2000s.

popularity, a new type of underground rap developed to take the place of the old and alternative hip-hop styles. The new underground rap was created by artists who wanted to separate themselves from the corporate media connections and sponsorships that mainstream hip-hop had made. These artists often had political reasons for staying underground. Many felt as if corporations and government entities were controlling what was said. Going underground was one way to gain the freedom to express themselves in any way they wanted and to reach audiences who were not necessarily buying records or digital music. In 2013, Lauryn Hill, a rapper who had won Grammys for her singing and songwriting but was also convicted of tax evasion, explained her shift to underground rap:

> For the past several years, I have remained what others would consider underground. I did this in order to build a community of people, like-minded in their desire for freedom and the right to pursue their goals and lives without being manipulated and controlled by a media protected military industrial complex with a completely different agenda.[1]

Hill also said that part of the reason for her tax evasion was the need to remove herself and her family from the manipulation and exploitation of the mainstream music industry and still provide for their needs.

Many underground rappers are committed to political and social causes, such as antiwar activities or human rights. These stances are not always popular with mainstream record labels or corporate sponsors. When

Lauryn Hill performs at a human rights concert in Brooklyn, New York City, in 2014.

faced with the choice of quieting their own opinions to stay with mainstream music production or going out on their own and expressing themselves, underground rappers decided to leave the visible hip-hop music scene. They use rap music to educate and inform people instead of turning them into consumers. Some of these underground rappers, including Mos Def and Talib Kweli, as well as Hill, were in the mainstream and enjoyed popular success and celebrity but then decided to go underground to regain their artistic individuality.

Underground rappers are usually independent artists who are not tied to a big record label and the marketing and promotion that comes with it. They sometimes sign with

MOS DEF

Mos Def, now known as Yasiin Bey, is a hip-hop recording artist, actor, and activist. He started rapping at the age of nine, and acting at the age of 14, appearing in movies, including The Italian Job, and also on Broadway. His music career has sometimes been second to his acting, but he has several albums that have been underground hits and has also collaborated with rapper Talib Kweli. He also worked on the Black Jack Johnson project, which tried to reinvigorate rock music, especially the rap-rock hybrid. Def has also used his visibility to protest the government's response after Hurricane Katrina in 2005 and the Jena Six incident in 2007, when six black teenagers were convicted of beating a white teen in Jena, Louisiana, after a period of racial tension. In 2016, Mos Def announced that he was retiring from the entertainment industry.

independent labels or use social media to advertise digital music or mixtapes that can be downloaded for free. Performances generally take place in public places, restaurants, and open-air venues. The artist does everything: sells tickets and merchandise, such as T-shirts and mixtapes, and generates publicity on Facebook and other social media sites.

> "Hip-hop is here to empower people. Hip-hop is here to reconnect us with our humanity."[2]
>
> —Brother Ali, hip-hop artist, community activist, and member of the Rhymesayers Entertainment hip-hop collective

Underground's Unusual Relatives

Underground hip-hop and rap also created some distinctive and interesting subgroups. One example is nerdcore, a type of hip-hop that includes themes, lyrics, and subject matter that appeal to nerds. These songs include lyrics about science fiction, anime, role-playing, video games, science, and computers. Some nerdcore rappers include Mega Ran, who teamed up with Richie Branson to produce the song "Zombies Ate My Neighbors," based on an old video game. Artist MC Frontalot actually gave nerdcore its name with his 2000 song "Nerdcore Hip-Hop." Adam WarRock is a former lawyer whose nerdcore songs "Magneto Was

Right" and "That Was Cyclops" are based on Marvel superhero characters.

There is also a genre of underground rap known as horrorcore. Whereas hip-hop had always dealt with the harder aspects of life in the inner city, such as violence and death, horrorcore goes further with these themes. Horrorcore's themes include Satanism, the supernatural, suicide, murder, and the kinds of violence found in slasher horror movies. The first acknowledged horrorcore single, "Assassins," was part of a Geto Boys album from 1988. Some horrorcore songs come from popular slasher movies, such as "A Nightmare on My Street" and "Are You Ready for Freddy" from the movie *A Nightmare on Elm Street*. These songs were included in the sound track for the fourth

REVENGE OF THE NERDCORE

In October 2016, on the popular television quiz show *Jeopardy!*, host Alex Trebek insulted the nerdcore hip-hop genre followers after a contestant told him she was a fan of rap music about video games and science fiction. "It's called 'nerdcore' hip-hop. It's people who identify as nerdy, rapping about the things they love," the contestant, Susan Cole, described to Trebek. The game host joked in response: "Losers, in other words." The nerdcore rapper Mega Ran responded via Twitter. "Nobody likes a know-it-all. . . . But Susan got the last laugh." The rapper continued, "20 grand cash and you're good at all my shows, you don't even have to ask."[3]

Freddy movie and included rapping by Robert Englund himself, who played Freddy. Other horrorcore rappers include Insane Clown Posse, Flatlinerz, Gravediggaz, and Kung Fu Vampire. Horrorcore has been seen as the darkest side of hip-hop and is generally not popular with

> "If you take Stephen King or Wes Craven and you throw them on a rap beat, that's who I am."[4]
>
> —Horrorcore rapper Mars

Violent J of Insane Clown Posse gets the crowd excited during a Halloween show in Detroit, Michigan.

mainstream hip-hop fans, although it continues to have many followers.

Failure Is the New Success

Most musicians and music producers consider the digital mistakes in music recording, such as skips, pops, and scratches, to be failures. But another new genre of hip-hop, called glitch hop, is built from the musical effects of digital failures. These glitches produce sound effects such as electrical hums, distortion, hisses and scratches from vinyl records, and other hardware noise. Glitch hop artists include MC Push Button Objects, the Glitch Mob, and Pretty Lights.

Glitch hop fused with dubstep, a type of electronic dance music that originated in London, to create wonky music. Wonky music is based on irregular beats that sound chaotic, bass lines that have the failure glitches of glitch hop, and other glitch features such as skips. Wonky music is different from glitch hop because it has richer melodies with synthesizer effects that are unstable and fluctuating. Similar to glitch hop, wonky music has never had wide popularity, but it does have a strong underground and alternative following.

Glitch hop performed by the Glitch Mob includes rapping done over glitch effects, with additional hip-hop elements such as beat repeating and skipping.

As hip-hop entered the new millennium, it regained some of its political and social voice. Hip-hop also became an acknowledged influence on many other types of music, especially pop. But where is hip-hop headed as it evolves and moves into the future?

8 HIP-HOP'S
FUTURE

As a genre, mainstream hip-hop was declining by 2005. Alternative and underground rap and hip-hop were providing a way for newer artists to explore the genre. It also gave them a way to voice their political and social positions, especially **when** they were different from those of the big record producers and labels. But mainstream hip-hop itself was no longer fresh with new artists and techniques and had grown stale. Many long-term hip-hop fans were looking elsewhere for new music. Alternative hip-hop genres were also fostering a marketing model based on free downloads or mixtapes instead of having fans buy albums or expensive concert tickets.

Macklemore topped the charts in 2013 despite releasing music independently and forgoing the marketing power of a record label.

A HISTORY OF DIGITAL MUSIC SHARING

In the late 1990s, the way people obtained and listened to music changed. Music was previously bought in the form of records, cassette tapes, and CDs. But with the invention of the MP3 file, suddenly music could be bought and shared digitally, with no hard copies at all. People soon discovered they could download and share music illegally, either by buying CDs and then making them into digital files to share for free, or by downloading other people's copies of albums and songs. Sites such as Napster and Limewire allowed users free access to music. This had a terrible financial effect on record companies, which lost huge amounts of money since fans were no longer paying for music. Since then, many online music file sharing sites have been sued or shut down. Some individuals who have illegally downloaded music have also been sued by record companies. Music file sharing is still controversial, with some artists fighting against it and others using it as a way to reach more fans.

The Decline of Hip-Hop

Music critics have had many reasons for declaring that hip-hop is either dead or dying. They are quick to define the trend as only concerning mainstream hip-hop, not the international or underground versions. Some critics feel the decline of hip-hop is the same decline that affects any music type that originated with African Americans and was taken over by white performers. As writer Tiffanie Drayton said in the article "8 Reasons Why Hip-Hop / R&B Is Dead" in *Clutch* magazine,

The history of American music has told the same story over and over again: Black people create a musical style or genre,

Some music critics feel white performers can work in black-generated musical genres, but they are rarely innovative and do not enhance the genre, so it slowly withers away.

Other critics believe hip-hop has not evolved culturally with the times. It is still dominated by men and often expresses negative attitudes toward women and the LGBT community, even though these groups now have greater spending power and a more accepted place in society than they once did. Women are still sometimes portrayed as nothing more than sexual objects, and some hip-hop lyrics contain negative references to gays and lesbians. By ignoring, insulting, or criticizing these groups, hip-hop artists may have reduced their potential audience.

Another issue that has made things difficult for hip-hop music is the practice of sampling—using parts of other tracks and songs and rapping over them—and a new attention to legal rights. Hip-hop was born through the practice of DJs talking over recorded song tracks, and many of the hip-hop songs that were recorded and sold as albums used pieces of these other existing songs.

Pharrell Williams, *left*, and Robin Thicke, *right*, had legal issues surrounding their song "Blurred Lines" and the use of sampling.

However, in 1991, a US district court case, *Grand Upright Music, Ltd. v. Warner Bros. Records, Inc.*, required performers to stop using samples freely and required them to obtain permission in advance for using other artists' songs. Many

performers are now either suing hip-hop artists who use
their music without permission or are being sued because
they themselves have used them. Sampling legally and
gaining rights to other tracks is expensive. Prices can

range up to $10,000 per portion of music. Using legal samples is so expensive that it is now difficult to produce new hip-hop songs that use a large number of samples.

The decline of sampling has not only changed the sound of hip-hop but also taken some of its political and social messages away. As Hank Shocklee, a producer for the rap group Public Enemy, said, "A lot of the records that were being sampled were socially conscious, socially relevant records, and that has a way of shaping the lyrics that you're going to write in conjunction with them."[2] One of the reasons why underground rappers have been able to continue using unauthorized samples in their music is that they circulate their songs on free mixtapes. In doing so, they are technically not receiving any revenue from their music, which exempts them from the district court's ruling. The publicity and marketing value of these mixtapes and the samples used have allowed new artists to enter the hip-hop genre. The practice provides room for experimentation with the

> "Hip-hop is the streets. Hip-hop is a couple of elements that it comes from back in the days . . . that feel of music with urgency that speaks to you. It speaks to your livelihood and it's not compromised. It's blunt. It's raw, straight off the street— from the beat to the voice to the words."[3]
>
> —Nas

music, even when performers do not have the cash to get official permission for the samples they use.

Hip-Hop's Developing Voices

Hip-hop is far from dead as a musical genre. Some artists continue to develop it, including international hip-hop artists, such as K'naan, Shing02, and M.I.A., or new US artists, such as Lil Yachty. Some groups, such as Killah Priest, Awdazcate, and Jay IDK, are recording more classic styles of hip-hop, with familiar beats but a futuristic style. Killah Priest, whose real name is Walter Reed, is affiliated with the Wu-Tang Clan. His hip-hop music features spiritual lyrics with many religious references

KANYE WEST

Kanye West is a producer turned rapper who has also become a celebrity and an entrepreneur. In addition to his considerable creative output, he is well-known for making outrageous statements, as well as being married to reality television star Kim Kardashian. He got his major break by working as a producer for Jay Z and later for rapper Ludacris and singer Beyoncé. While working for other artists, West wrote his own music and recorded a demo, ultimately signing with Jay Z's label Roc-A-Fella Records. He has since won several Grammy Awards. He has also launched his own line of designer clothing and shoes and started the Kanye West Foundation to work with high school dropouts. He continues to record songs, including "New Slaves," which he promoted by projecting a video of himself singing the song onto the sides of 66 buildings in ten cities. The song is controversial because of its explicit lyrics and its examples of forms of slavery that still exist today.

and symbols. His music is considered controversial because of the political subject matter he covers in his lyrics. Killah Priest is also a member of the Black Hebrew Israelites. These Jewish African Americans believe they are the direct descendants of the ancient biblical Israelites who lived in the Holy Land of the Middle East.

Shingo Annen, known as Shing02, is a Japanese hip-hop artist and producer. Because he grew up in several different Western cities, he is one of the few rappers who can compose his music entirely in Japanese or English. He is known for songs that address Japanese issues such as ethnicity, education, and sexual exploitation. His music blends the sounds of traditional Japanese music with reggae and jazz.

Rapper Lil Yachty is a rising hip-hop star, known for his trademark red-beaded hair and his nasal, high-pitched voice, which even he admits sounds like a cartoon. He became popular after his song "1Night" was used in a comedy sketch and gained the attention of viewers across the United States. His songs feature comical lyrics and unusual, unique melodies. He also appeared as a model in rapper Kanye West's Yeezy Season 3 fashion show in 2016.

Lil Yachty first gained recognition in 2015 with his debut songs.

JAY IDK

Jay IDK, which stands for "Ignorantly Delivering Knowledge," released a hip-hop album in 2016 called *Empty Bank*. Its songs talk about the importance of financial literacy and the problems faced by rappers who go from being poor to having money overnight. Jay IDK aspires to be the first rapper to win the Nobel Peace Prize:

> *I just know that I talk about things that you should really pay attention to and understand. And I think that one day I will make an album that could open that door. Rap is such a part of pop culture now. . . . There's a lot of things that I try to do with my stuff that's unprecedented. Some stuff works, some stuff is crazy.*[4]

These hip-hop artists show that as a genre, hip-hop is still developing new voices. Some of these artists use their music for serious commentaries about politics and culture, whereas others provide entertainment and link themselves to consumerism. Hip-hop still covers the full range of intentions and styles.

Hip-Hop beyond the Music Industry

Hip-hop was partly born from an African-American tradition of using songs as a way to protest and even fight against inequality, including antislavery songs of the Civil War era and songs of protest from the civil rights era. In 2015 and 2016, it followed in that tradition as part of the Black Lives Matter campaign. Many rappers used their music to speak out against racial oppression in the wake of highly publicized police killings of black people, including Michael Brown in Ferguson, Missouri, in 2014 and Freddie Gray in Baltimore, Maryland, in 2015. It also moved hip-hop further away from its modern stance as a feel-good commercial genre and back to its street roots.

In August 2015, Janelle Monáe's Wondaland Records collective of rap artists released a single called "Hell You Talmbout," which the group had performed live during a march against police brutality in Philadelphia, Pennsylvania. The song was intended to be a rallying cry for Black Lives Matter and has been used that way since its release. Monáe said,

This song is a vessel. It carries the unbearable anguish of millions. We recorded it to channel the pain, fear, and trauma caused by the ongoing

TEF POE

US rapper Tef Poe is known for his activism. After the riots in Ferguson, Missouri, in August 2014, which followed the police shooting of unarmed black teenager Michael Brown, Poe was one of the leaders of the early Black Lives Matter movement. He also started his own organization, HandsUp United, dedicated to social justice. He is said to have coined the phrase "This ain't your grandparents' civil rights movement."[5] Poe traveled to the White House to meet with President Barack Obama about issues such as race, police brutality, and the Ferguson riots. He also traveled to Geneva, Switzerland, where he delivered a speech bringing attention to the aftermath of Brown's death. The police officer was not charged with any crimes. Poe later released a single about the Ferguson riots called "War Cry."

Monáe is one of the hip-hop artists heavily involved in the Black Lives Matter movement.

slaughter of our brothers and sisters. We recorded it to challenge the indifference, disregard, and negligence of all who remain quiet about this issue. Silence is our enemy. Sound is our weapon.[6]

In addition to finding a fresh voice for political and social action, hip-hop has also found its way into the academic world, beginning with Harvard University's Hip Hop Archive and Research Institute, established in 2002. In 2014, Professor Darin Flynn of Canada's University of Calgary debuted a college course on rap linguistics. The course uses hip-hop music to show how the English language has evolved in hip-hop and how sounds, words, grammar, and meaning are used and manipulated in hip-hop lyrics. Flynn explained that because rap doesn't use harmony or melody, the music is more about rhythm, adding, "[Rappers] also rhyme in interesting ways and [convey] interesting meanings."[7] This class, and others like it, demonstrates that hip-hop has indeed become part of the popular musical culture of the United States.

Moving Forward

Hip-hop has evolved quickly in terms of musical genres. In less than 50 years, it has moved from a local, neighborhood musical style, practiced at block parties,

Hip-hop has become such a large part of American culture that high schools and colleges are teaching rap linguistics and other aspects of the genre.

expressing the experiences and perspectives of people living in the inner city, to a billion-dollar music industry. And even though many music critics feel hip-hop has sold out to big corporations and a consumer lifestyle, there are plenty of underground and independent hip-hop artists who are proving them wrong. Hip-hop continues to be an

outlet for those who feel their voices aren't being heard. It is also an expression of a piece of US and world culture and a way to protest. As long as hip-hop continues its evolution, through fresh voices and experimental forms, it will continue to be a vibrant and living musical genre.

TIMELINE

1973

DJ Kool Herc deejays his sister's birthday party and uses two turntables to extend the breaks on records.

1975

DJ Grand Wizard Theodore starts the turntable technique of scratching.

1979

The Sugarhill Gang records the single "Rapper's Delight."

1981

The rock group Blondie releases the song "Rapture," which features rapping.

1984

Radio station KDAY in Los Angeles, California, becomes the first rap-only radio station.

1987

Salt-N-Pepa's song "Push It" is the one of the first rap songs to be nominated for a Grammy Award.

1988

MTV music channel creates a program called *Yo! MTV Raps*, showcasing rap music.

1990

The cover of *Newsweek* magazine features the rap star Tone Lōc and articles about "rap rage."

1991

The US district court case *Grand Upright Music, Ltd. v. Warner Bros. Records, Inc.*, requires performers to stop using samples without permission.

1992

Rap music becomes the sound track for the racial tensions leading to the Los Angeles race riots.

1996

Rapper Tupac Shakur is killed in a drive-by shooting in Las Vegas.

2007

Grandmaster Flash and the Furious Five is the first rap group to be inducted into the Rock and Roll Hall of Fame.

2011

Rapper Common performs at a poetry reading at the White House with President Obama.

2014

Professor Darin Flynn of Canada's University of Calgary debuts a college course on rap linguistics.

2015

Janelle Monáe's Wondaland Records collective releases the single "Hell You Talmbout."

2016

Jay Z performs at a benefit concert for presidential candidate Hillary Clinton; rap music is used for political expression during the Black Lives Matter movement.

ESSENTIAL
FACTS

Hip-hop originated in the urban areas of New York City as an expression of what life was like there. It soon spread across the country, inspiring many subgenres. This music form became a commercial success and established itself within the mainstream music of the United States and eventually the world. It continues to serve as an outlet for political and social commentary by racial and ethnic minorities and other marginalized communities. Its themes of violence, drugs, and poverty, as well as the use of explicit lyrics and subject matter, have made it controversial.

KEY PLAYERS AND TRENDS

- DJ Grand Wizard Theodore perfected the technique of scratching while deejaying in the 1970s.

- DJ Kool Herc is credited with creating break beat hip-hop music in the 1970s.

- Grandmaster Flash and the Furious Five was the first hip-hop group inducted into the Rock and Roll Hall of Fame. The group released "The Message," which was seen as the beginning of hip-hop's social consciousness in the 1980s.

- Afrika Bambaataa was one of the first rappers to become famous outside of the United States in the 1980s.

- Tupac Shakur was a well-known gangsta rapper in the 1990s who was eventually killed in Las Vegas. His music was violent and controversial.

- Jay Z and Eminem became famous as hardcore rappers in the 1990s.

- Run-D.M.C. collaborated with Aerosmith to launch a new type of hip-hop called rap rock.

- Kanye West is a producer turned rapper most known for his work done in the 2000s and 2010s.

- The Glitch Mob helped make glitch hop popular in the 2000s.

- Lil Jon & the East Side Boyz made crunk popular with their song "Get Low" in 2003.

LEGACY

Hip-hop's legacy is as a voice for those who live in urban, low-income areas and for the African-American community. It continues to address political and social issues while it entertains.

QUOTE

"Hip-hop is here to empower people. Hip-hop is here to reconnect us with our humanity."

–Brother Ali, hip-hop artist, community activist, and member of the Rhymesayers Entertainment hip-hop collective

GLOSSARY

BACK-SPINNING
Moving a record backward to repeat a phrase of music or lyrics.

BRUTALITY
Cruel, harsh, and violent treatment of another person.

DISILLUSION
To cause dissatisfaction or ruin someone's hopes.

EXPLICIT
Open in the depiction of nudity, sexuality, violence, or drug use.

GANGSTA RAP
A type of rap music with lyrics featuring the violence and drug use of urban gang life.

GENRE
A specific type of music, film, or writing.

GHETTO
A section of a town or city in which people of a certain race, religion, or ethnic group are forced to live.

MAINSTREAM
A dominant trend in art or music, widely known and accepted as conventional.

MIXTAPE
A compilation of unreleased tracks, freestyle rap music, and DJ mixes of songs.

PHASING

Changing the speeds of turntables to create sound effects.

PRODUCER

The person who supervises the sampling, mixing, and recording of music and also guides the performers.

PSYCHEDELIC

Influenced by the drug culture of hallucinations and altered perceptions.

SAMPLING

The process of using prerecorded sounds to create a new piece of music.

SUPPRESS

To hold something back or intentionally avoid thinking about painful or unacceptable subjects.

SYNTHESIZER

A machine that uses amplifiers and filters to create sound electronically.

TURNTABLISM

The art of manipulating sounds and creating music using record turntables and a DJ mixer.

UNDERGROUND

Relating to a social or artistic world that is different or separate from the main part of society.

ADDITIONAL
RESOURCES

SELECTED BIBLIOGRAPHY

"The Art of Turntablism." *PBS History Detectives*. PBS, n.d. Web. 9 Oct. 2016.

Chang, Jeff. *Can't Stop Won't Stop: A History of the Hip-Hop Generation*. New York: Picador, 2005. Print.

Hardy, Ernest, and August Brown. "Los Angeles Riots: Gangsta Rap Foretold Them and Grew after Them." *Los Angeles Times*. Los Angeles Times, 2 May 2012. Web. 9 Oct. 2016.

Kamer, Foster. "The 40 Biggest Hip-Hop Moments in Pop Culture History." *Complex*. Complex, 26 Mar. 2013. Web. 9 Oct. 2016.

FURTHER READINGS

Berlatsky, Noah. *Opposing Viewpoints: Rap Music*. Farmington Hills, MI: Greenhaven, 2012. Print.

Matty B with Travis Thrasher. *That's a Rap*. New York: Gallery, 2016. Print.

WEBSITES

To learn more about Hip-Hop Insider, visit **abdobooklinks.com**. These links are routinely monitored and updated to provide the most current information available.

FOR MORE INFORMATION

For more information on this subject, contact or visit the following organizations:

HIP-HOP CAUCUS
20 F Street NW, 7th Floor
Washington, DC 20001
877-822-7019
http://www.hiphopcaucus.org
Hip-Hop Caucus uses hip-hop culture as a way to campaign for voting, environmental issues, civil and human rights, and economic empowerment.

HIP-HOP FOR CHANGE
2313 San Pablo
Oakland, CA 94612
415-202-4817
http://www.hiphopforchange.org
Hip-Hop for Change seeks to use hip-hop for education and community building, as well as providing a way for people who identify with hip-hop culture to express their true voices, selves, and culture.

HIP-HOP 4 LIFE
225 West 35th Street, Suite 301
New York, NY 10001
212-967-6730
http://hiphop4lifeinc.org
Hip-Hop 4 Life's mission is to help create strong youth leaders who are committed to personal growth and academic success.

SOURCE NOTES

CHAPTER 1. THE BIRTH OF THE SCRATCH

1. Billy Jam. "Creator of the Scratch: Grand Wizard Theodore." *Hip Hop Slam*. Hip Hop Slam, 9 Oct. 2016. Web. 2 Feb. 2017.

2. Ibid.

3. Adam Krims. *Rap Music and the Poetics of Identity*. Cambridge, UK: Cambridge UP, 2000. *Google Book Search*. 2 Feb. 2017.

4. Abbie Fentress Swanson. "The South Bronx: Where Hip-Hop Was Born." *WNYC*. New York Public Radio, 2 Aug. 2010. Web. 2 Feb. 2017.

CHAPTER 2.THE ROOTS OF HIP-HOP

1. Faisal Ahmed. "The True Meaning of Hip-Hop Culture by Afrika Bambaataa." *Bomb Hip-Hop Magazine* 38 (Mar. 1995). *Bomb Hip-Hop*. Web. 2 Feb. 2017.

2. History.com Staff. "Hip-hop Is Born at a Birthday Party in the Bronx." *History.com*. A+E Networks, 2009. Web. 2 Feb. 2017.

3. Jennifer Lee. "An Effort to Honor the Birthplace of Hip-Hop." *New York Times*. New York Times, 23 July 2007. Web. 2 Feb. 2017.

CHAPTER 3. MAINSTREAM MUSIC

1. Joe Lynch. "35 Years Ago, Sugarhill Gang's 'Rapper's Delight' Made Its First Chart Appearance." *Billboard*. Billboard, 13 Oct. 2014. Web. 2 Feb. 2017.

2. "The Golden Age of Hip Hop." *TV Tropes*. TV Tropes, n.d. Web. 2 Feb. 2017.

3. Christopher R. Weingarten. "Run-D.M.C. on Receiving Rap's First Grammy Lifetime Achievement Award." *Rolling Stone*. Rolling Stone, 11 Feb. 2016. Web. 2 Feb. 2017.

4. "Public Enemy." *Rock & Roll Hall of Fame*. Rock & Roll Hall of Fame, n.d. Web. 2 Feb. 2017.

CHAPTER 4. HIP-HOP GOES POLITICAL

1. "Grandmaster Flash—The Message Lyrics." *LyricsFreak*. LyricsFreak, 2017. Web. 2 Feb 2017.

2. Michel Marriott. "Hard-Core Rap Lyrics Stir Backlash." *New York Times*. New York Times, 15 Aug. 1993. Web. 2 Feb. 2017.

3. "Toddy Tee—Batterram Lyrics." *AZLyrics.biz*. AZ Lyrics, n.d. Web. 2 Feb 2017.

4. History.com. "Riots Erupt in Los Angeles." *History.com*. A+E Networks, 2010. Web. 2 Feb. 2017.

5. Ernest Hardy and August Brown. "Los Angeles Riots: Gangsta Rap Foretold Them and Grew After Them." *Los Angeles Times*. Los Angeles Times, 2 May 2012. Web. 2 Feb. 2017.

6. "Grandmaster Flash—The Message Lyrics." *LyricsFreak*. LyricsFreak, 2017. Web. 2 Feb 2017.

7. "The 50 Greatest Hip-Hop Songs of All Time." *Rolling Stone*. Rolling Stone, 5 Dec. 2012. Web. 2 Feb. 2017.

CHAPTER 5. EAST COAST VERSUS WEST COAST

1. Allison Samuels. "Suge Knight Is Back in Business." *Newsweek*. Newsweek, 22 April 2001. Web. 2 Feb. 2017.

2. "Eminem Quotes." *BrainyQuote*. BrainyQuote, 2017. Web. 2 Feb. 2017.

SOURCE NOTES
CONTINUED

CHAPTER 6. WORLD MUSIC

1. "Afrika Bambaataa Quotes." *BrainyQuote*. BrainyQuote, 2017. Web. 2 Feb. 2017.

2. Jimmy Wang. "Now Hip-Hop, Too, Is Made in China." *New York Times*. New York Times, 23 Jan. 2009. Web. 2 Feb. 2017.

CHAPTER 7. NEW HIP-HOP

1. Timothy Alexander Guzman. "Why Does the Music Industry Keep 'Underground Hip-Hop Music' Underground?" *Global Research*. Global Research, 25 Oct. 2013. Web. 2 Feb. 2017.

2. Ruth Blatt. "Beyond Bravado: Underground Rappers Resurrect Hip-hop's Roots as Protest Music." *Forbes*. Forbes, 17 Oct. 2013. Web. 2 Feb. 2017.

3. Nerisha Penrose. "Alex Trebek Calls Nerdcore Rap Fans 'Losers'; MC Chris and Mega Ran Respond." *Billboard*. Billboard, 13 Oct. 2016. Web. 2 Feb. 2017.

4. Kirsten Jusewicz-Haidle. "Juggalos—Transcript." *Life of the Law*. Life of the Law, 23 Feb. 2016. Web. 2 Feb. 2017.

CHAPTER 8. HIP-HOP'S FUTURE

1. Tiffanie Drayton. "8 Reasons Why Hip-Hop / R&B Is Dead." *Clutch*. Sutton New Media, 2014. Web. 2 Feb. 2017.

2. Erik Nielson. "Did the Decline of Sampling Cause the Decline of Political Hip-hop?" *Atlantic*. Atlantic, 18 Sept. 2013. Web. 2 Feb. 2017.

3. "Hip-Hop Quotes." *BrainyQuote*. BrainyQuote, 2017. Web. 2 Feb. 2017.

4. Lanre Bakare. "St. Louis Rapper Turned Activist Tef Poe Releases Shooting Protest Song 'War Cry.'" *Guardian*. Guardian News and Media, 12 Nov. 2014. Web. 2 Feb. 2017.

5. Jessica McKinney. "Meet Jay IDK, The DMV's Breakout MC Here to Change the Game." *Vibe*. Vibe, 12 Sept. 2016. Web. 2 Feb. 2017.

6. Alexander Billet. "The New Anthems of Resistance: Hip-Hop and Black Lives Matter." *In These Times*. In These Times, 21 Aug. 2015. Web. 2 Feb. 2017.

7. Jessica Patterson. "Rap Lyrics the Topic of New Linguistics Course at the University of Calgary." *Metro*. Free Daily News Group, 7 Aug. 2014. Web. 2 Feb. 2017.

INDEX

ABOUT THE AUTHOR

Marcia Amidon Lusted has written 135 books and more than 500 magazine articles for young readers on topics such as history, biography, science, and literature. She is also an editor, a musician, and a certified permaculturist. She lives in New Hampshire.